Gigglers

ANIMAL JOKES

Toby Reynolds

Illustrated by
Andrew Pinder

For Samuel, my most favourite penguin,
love Uncle Toby

Scholastic Children's Books,
Euston House, 24 Eversholt Street
London NW1 1DB

A division of Scholastic Ltd
London ~ New York ~ Toronto ~ Sydney ~ Auckland
Mexico City ~ New Delhi ~ Hong Kong

First published in the UK by Scholastic Ltd, 2017

Text by Toby Reynolds
Illustrations by Andrew Pinder

© Scholastic Children's Books, 2017

ISBN 978 1407 16562 2

Printed and bound by CPI Group (UK) Ltd, Croydon, CR0 4YY

2 4 6 8 10 9 7 5 3 1

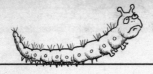

Contents

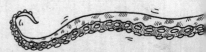

Funny Farms

Q. What did the horse say when he finished his meal?
A. That's the last straw!

Q. What is the difference between a horse and a duck?
A. One goes quick and the other goes quack!

Q. What did the horse say when it fell over?
A. "I've fallen and I can't giddy up!"

Q. Why did the horse eat with its mouth open?
A. Because it had bad stable manners.

Q. Why did the pony have to gargle?
A. Because it was a little horse!

Q. What do you call a horse that lives at the farm next door?
A. A neigh-bour!

Q. Why did the thrill-seeking farmer stand behind the horse?
A. He was hoping to get a kick out of it.

Q. What kind of farm animal goes OOM?
A. A cow walking backwards!

Q. Why did the farmer tell the geese to be quiet?
A. He was tired of their fowl language.

Q. What's a cow's favourite city?
A. Moo York!

Q. What is the difference between a chicken and an elephant?
A. An elephant can get chicken pox, but a chicken can't get elephant pox.

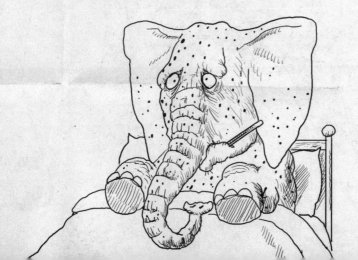

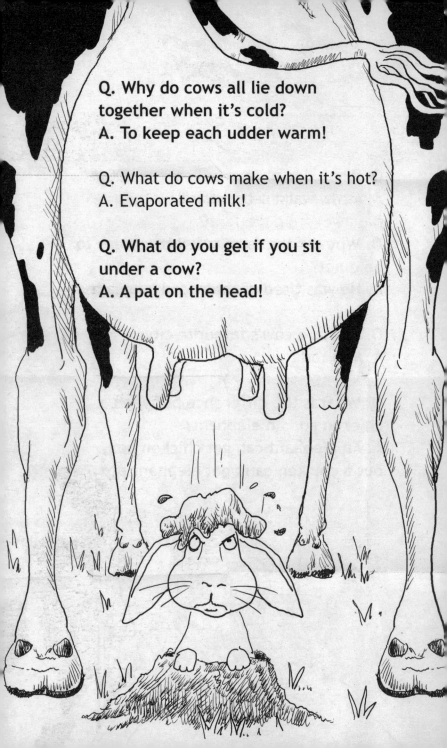

Q. What happened to the cow that ran away from the farm?
A. He was never herd of again!

Q. What did the mummy cow say to the baby cow?
A. It's pasture bedtime.

Knock, knock.
Who's there?
Cows go.
Cows go who?
Cows go moo, not who!

9

Q. How do farmers count their cows?
A. They use a cow-culator.

Q. Why do cows love joke books?
A. Because they love to be amoosed!

Q. Why is it hard to have a conversation with a goat?
A. Because they keep butting in!

Q. What does a cow read every morning?
A. A moos-paper.

10

Q. What do you call a goat
dressed like a clown?
A. A silly billy.

Q. When did the goat realize he
was a goat?
A. When he was just a little kid.

Q. What do you call a thief that
steals pigs?
A. A ham burglar!

ROB 1

Q. What is a pig's favourite ballet?
A. Swine Lake!

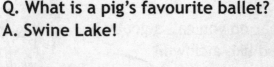

Q. What do you call a pig with six eyes?
A. A piiiiiig.

Knock, Knock.
Who's there?
Oink, oink.
Oink, oink who?
Make up your mind – are you a pig or an owl?

Q. What is the fastest way to take a pig to hospital?
A. By ham-bulance!

Q. Is it true that pigs take two baths a day?
A. No, that story is just a load of hogwash.

Q. Why is a pig the best actor on the farm?
A. He loves to ham it up and hog all the attention.

Q. How did the farmer fit more pigs on his farm?
A. He built a sty-scraper!

Q. What is a pig's favourite Shakespeare play?
A. Hamlet.

Q. How do pig's explain the beginnings of the universe?
A. With the Pig Bang Theory.

Q. Why was the pig sacked from his job as a TV talk show host?
A. He turned out to be a big boar.

Q. What farm vehicles do pigs love to drive?
A. Pig-up trucks!

Q. What animal sounds like a sheep but isn't?
A. A baa-boon!

Q. How does the farmer greet the pigs at Christmas?
A. Merry Christmas to ewe!

Q. How many sheep does it take to knit a jumper?
A. Don't be silly – sheep can't knit!

Q. What do you call a sheep with no legs?
A. A cloud.

Q. **Where do sheep get their wool cut?**
A. **At the baa-baa shop!**

Q. Why was the sheep arrested on the motorway?
A. Because she did a ewe-turn!

Q. **Where does a sheep wash?**
A. **In the baa-th tub!**

Q. Where do sheep go on holiday?
A. To the baa-hamas.

Q. What did the ambitious sheep want to do?
A. Wool the world.

Q. What kind of car does a sheep dream of driving?
A. A Lamb-borghini.

Q. What was the sheep's favourite swimming style?
A. The baa-ckstroke!

Jungle Gags

Knock, knock.
Who's there?
Chimp.
Chimp who?
A chimp off the old block!

Q. How do monkeys get down the stairs?
A. They slide down the banana-ster!

Q. Why do gorillas have big nostrils?
A. Because they have big fingers!

Q. What do you call a monkey with
a banana in each ear?
A. Anything you want,
it can't hear you.

Knock, knock.
Who's there?
Gorilla.
Gorilla who?
Gorilla-d cheese for me, please!

Q. What kind of a key opens a banana?
A. A monkey!

Q. Why did the monkey like
the banana?
A. Because it had appeal!

Q. What do you call a monkey who's training to be a wizard?
A. Hairy Potter.

Q. Where do chimps get their gossip?
A. On the ape vine!

Q. How do you keep a monkey in suspense?
A. I'll tell you tomorrow.

Q. Why did the tiger lose at poker?
A. Because he was playing against a cheetah!

Q. What is the fiercest flower in the jungle?
A. A tiger lily!

Q. How is a tiger like an army sergeant?
A. They both wear stripes with pride.

Q. Who went into the tiger's den and came out alive?
A. The tiger!

Q. On which day of the week do tigers eat people?
A. Chews-day!

Q. What's the silliest name you can give a tiger?
A. Spot!

21

Potty Pets

Q. How did the cat feel after eating a duck?
A. A little down in the mouth!

Q. What is a cat's favourite TV programme?
A. The Mews at Ten!

Q. What did the cat do when he saw a mouse?
A. Made a feline for it!

Q. When is it bad luck to see a black cat?
A. When you're a mouse!

Ooops!

Q. What does a cat with stinky breath need?
A. Mouse wash!

Q. What happened to the cat that swallowed a ball of wool?
A. She had mittens!

Q. What do you call a cat that has just eaten a duck?
A. A duck-filled fatty puss!

Q. What has twelve legs, three tails and can't see?
A. Three blind mice!

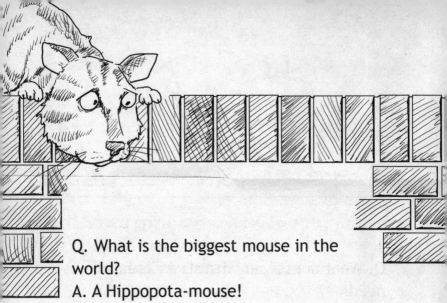

Q. What is the biggest mouse in the world?
A. A Hippopota-mouse!

Q. What do you give to a drowning mouse?
A. Mouse to mouse resuscitation!

Q. Why was the mouse afraid of the river?
A. Because of all the catfish.

Q. What is small, furry and brilliant at sword fighting?
A. A mouse-keteer!

Q. What goes dot, dot, dash, squeak?
A. Mouse code!

Q. How do mice celebrate when they move to a new home?
A. They throw a mouse-warming party!

Q. What kind of dog does Dracula have?
A. A bloodhound!

Q. What do you call a dog magician?
A. A Labracadabrador.

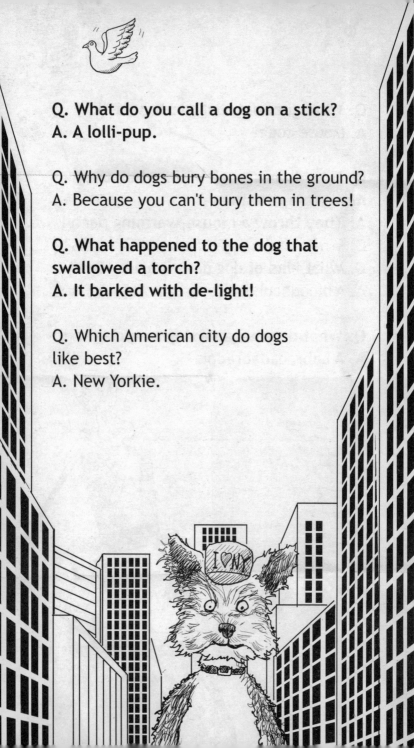

Q. What do you call a dog on a stick?
A. A lolli-pup.

Q. Why do dogs bury bones in the ground?
A. Because you can't bury them in trees!

Q. What happened to the dog that
swallowed a torch?
A. It barked with de-light!

Q. Which American city do dogs
like best?
A. New Yorkie.

Q. What did the cat say to the dog?
A. Check meow-t!

Q. **Where did the dog keep his car?**
A. **In the car bark.**

Q. **What kind of dog likes taking baths?**
A. **A shampoodle!**

Q. How does a dog stop watching a film?
A. By pressing the paws button.

Q. What do Dalmatians say after a
satisfying meal?
A. That really hit the spots!

Knock, knock.
Who's there?
Rabbit.
Rabbit who?
Rabbit up neatly – it's fragile!

Q. Why do Australian dogs cross the road twice?
A. Because they are always trying to fetch boomerangs!

Q. Why did the bald man put a rabbit on his head?
A. Because he wanted a head of hare!

Q. How do rabbits travel?
A. By hare-oplane.

Q. What did the rabbit give his girlfriend when he asked her to marry him?
A. A 14 carrot ring!

Q. Where do rabbits go after their wedding?
A. On their bunnymoon!

Q. What do you call a sunburnt rabbit?
A. A hot cross bunny.

Q. How do you know that eating carrots is good for your eyes?
A. Because you never see rabbits wearing glasses!

Q. How can you tell which rabbits are getting old?
A. Look for the grey hares.

Q. What's the difference between a healthy rabbit and an odd rabbit?
A. One is a fit bunny and the other is a bit funny!

Q. Why did the rabbit build herself a new house?
A. She was fed up with the hole thing!

Silly Sea Life

Q. Why are fish so well educated?
A. They are always in schools!

Q. What do you call a fish with no eyes?
A. A fsh!

Knock, knock.
Who's there?
Tuna.
Tuna who?
Tuna your banjo and you can
join our band!

Q. Which fish go to heaven when they die?
A. Angelfish.

Q. Who's the most frightening fish in the ocean?
A. Jack the kipper.

Q. Why do fish boots keep your ankles warm?
A. Because they have electric 'eels.

Q. What did the fish do when his piano sounded odd?
A. He called the piano tuna.

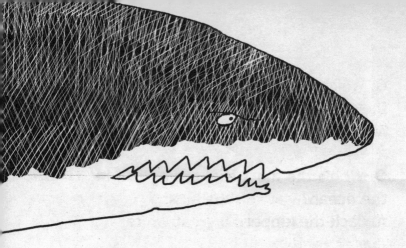

Q. Why did the shark cross the Great Barrier Reef?
A. To get to the other tide.

Q. What type of burgers do sharks love?
A. Quarter flounders with cheese.

Q. Why won't sharks eat clownfish?
A. They taste funny!

Q. What is a shark's favourite type of sandwich?
A. Peanut butter and jellyfish!

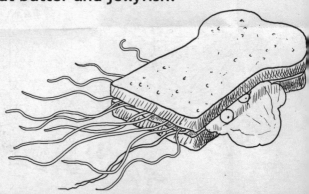

Q. Who delivers presents to sharks at Christmas?
A. Santa Jaws!

Q. What do you call the mushy stuff stuck between a great white shark's teeth?
A. Slow swimmers!

Q. Which sharks work on a building site?
A. Hammerhead sharks.

Q. How do you make a shark laugh?
A. Tell a whale of a tale.

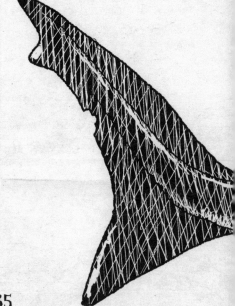

Q. What hobby does a shark like best?
A. Anything he can sink his teeth into.

Q. What did the shark say to the whale?
A. What are you blubbering on about?

Q. What did the dolphin say when he
bumped into the whale?
A. I didn't do it on porpoise!

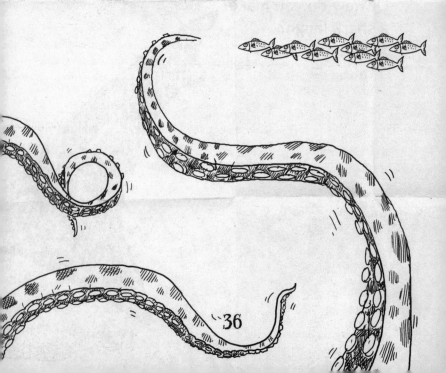

Q. Why did the fish want to be an astronaut?
A. He wanted to explore trout-er space!

Q. How do you make an octopus laugh?
A. With ten-tickles

Q. Did you hear about the two eels that had a race?
A. It ended in a tie!

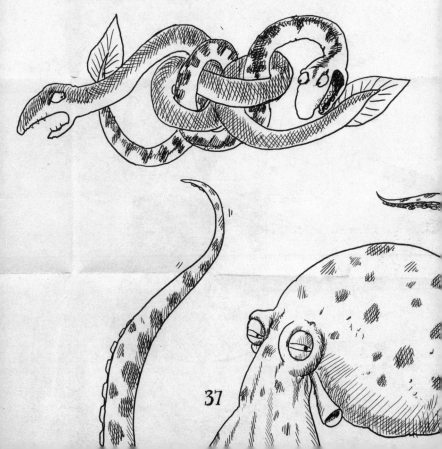

Q. Who held the baby octopus to ransom?
A. Squidnappers!

Q. Why are goldfish orange?
A. The water makes them rusty!

Q. What did the magician say to the fisherman?
A. Pick a cod, any cod!

Bonkers Birds

Q. Why do two sparrows in a nest never argue?
A. Because they don't want to fall out.

Q. What do sparrow families do on Saturday afternoon?
A. They go on peck-nics!

Q. What do you call a very rude pigeon?
A. A mockingbird!

Q. What time does a duck wake up?
A. At the quack of dawn!

Q. Who stole the soap?
A. The robber ducky!

Q. What was the goal of the
detective duck?
A. To quack the case

Knock, knock.
Who's there?
Quacker!
Quacker who?
Quacker another bad joke and
I'm leaving!

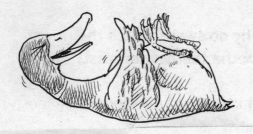

Q. What did the duck do after he read all these jokes?
A. He quacked up!

Q. **What says "Quick, Quick!"?**
A. **A duck with the hiccups.**

Q. What does a duck do first when making an omelette?
A. He quacks some eggs.

Q. **What do ducks watch on TV?**
A. **Duck-umentaries!**

Q. Why do swans watch the news?
A. For the feather forecast!

Q. Which side of a swan has the most feathers?
A. The outside!

Q. Why did the goose fly south for the winter?
A. Because it was too far to walk.

Q. What do you say at the reception of the fowl hotel?
A. I would like to chicken to my room please!

Q. What bird is helpful at dinner?
A. A swallow!

Q. What do you call a poorly eagle?
A. Illegal!

Q. What's the difference between bird flu and swine flu?

A. If you have bird flu, you need tweet-ment but if you have swine flu, you need oink-ment.

Q. Which bird can never catch its breath?

A. A puffin!

Q. How do you catch a unique puffin?

A. Unique up on it.

44

Q. How many birds does it take to change a light bulb?
A. Toucan do it.

Q. Why do hummingbirds hum?
A. Because they've forgotten the words!

Q. Why do seagulls live by the sea?
A. Because if they lived by the bay they would be bagels.

Comedy
Creepy Crawlies

Q. What do insects learn at school?
A. Moth-matics!

Q. What insect lives on nothing?
A. A moth, because it eats holes.

Q. What's the biggest moth in the world?
A. A mam-moth!

Q. What does a caterpillar do on New Year's Day?
A. It turns over a new leaf!

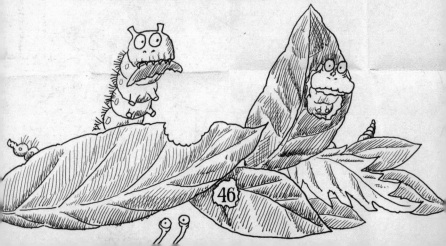

Q. What is the definition of
a caterpillar?
A. A worm in a fur coat!

Q. What has fifty legs but can't walk?
A. Half a centipede!

Q. What was the snail doing on the
motorway?
A. About a mile a day.

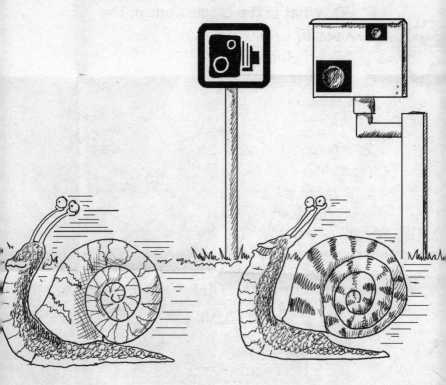

Knock, Knock.
Who's there?
Wood ant!
Wood ant who?
Don't be afraid. Wood ant harm a fly!

Q. Why was the baby ant confused?
A. Because all of his uncles were ants!

Q. What is the biggest ant in the world?
A. An eleph-ant!

Q. What kind of ant is good at maths?
A. An account-ant.

Q. What do you call 100-year-old ants?
A. Antiques.

Q. What do you call an ant that likes to be alone?
A. Independ-ant.

Q. What do you call an ant that skips school?
A. A tru-ant.

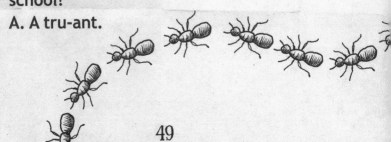

49

Q. What did the spider say to the fly on Halloween?
A. The web is the trick and you are the treat!

Q. Why don't anteaters get sick?
A. Because they are full of antibodies!

Q. What do you call an ant with frog legs?
A. An ant-phibian!

Q. What are spider webs good for?
A. Spiders!

Q. How do spiders communicate?
A. Through the World Wide Web.

Q. What kinds of doctors are like spiders?
A. Spin doctors!

Q. What does a spider do when he gets angry?
A. He goes up the wall!

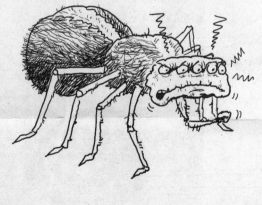

Q. What did the spider say when he broke his new web?
A. Darn it!

Q. Why did the spider get a job in IT?
A. She was a great web designer!

Q. Why did the spider buy a sports car?
A. So he could take it out for a spin!

Q. What do spiders eat in Paris?
A. French flies!

Q. What do you call two recently
married spiders?
A. Newly webs!

Q. Why do spiders have eight legs?
A. Because if they had six they would
be insects!

Q. Why do spiders spin webs?
A. Because they can't knit!

Q. What is a spider's favourite day?
A. Fly-day!

Q. What is a spider's favourite sport?
A. Fly fishing!

Slapstick Savannah

Q. Why do cheetahs always eat raw meat?
A. Because they don't know how to cook.

Q. Why are elephants such bad dancers?
A. Because they have two left feet!

Q. What's big and grey and protects you from the rain?
A. An umbrella-phant!

Q. Why did the leopard hide in the tall grass?
A. He didn't want to be spotted.

Q. What's the difference between African elephants and Indian Elephants?
A. About 3,000 miles.

Q. What's as big as an elephant, but weighs nothing?
A. An elephant's shadow.

Q. What do you call an elephant that never takes a bath?
A. A smelly-phant!

Q. Why did the elephant cross the road?
A. Because it was the chicken's day off!

Q. What's big and grey and flies upwards?
A. An ele-copter!

Q. What do you call an elephant that didn't understand any of these jokes?
A. Dumbo!

Q. What's green and hangs from trees?
A. Giraffe snot!

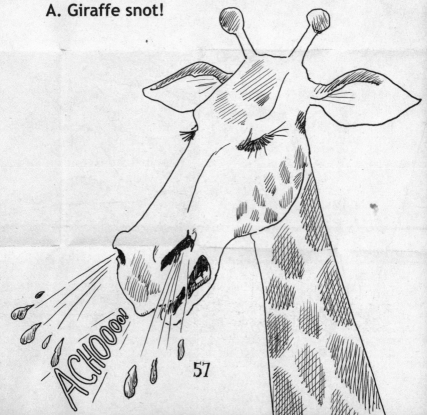

Q. Why are giraffes slow to apologize?
A. It takes them a while to swallow their pride.

Q. Why was the giraffe late?
A. Because he got caught in a giraffic jam!

Q. Why don't giraffes like to go to the playground?
A. Because the monkeys use them as slides.

Q. What's the difference between an injured lion and a wet day?
A. One pours with rain, the other roars with pain!

Knock, knock.
Who's there?
Omar.
Omar who?
Omar goodness, there's a huge lion behind you!

Q. What does a lion say to his pride before they go hunting?
A. Let us prey.

Q. How does a lion sail a boat?
A. He uses r-oars.

Q. What do you call a lion wearing a flowery dress?
A. A dandelion.

Q. What is a lion's favourite food?
A. Baked beings!

Q. Why was the lion-tamer fined?
A. He parked on a yellow lion!

Arctic Antics

Q. What kind of fish do penguins catch at night?
A. Starfish.

Q. What did one emperor penguin say to the other?
A. Nothing, they just gave each other the cold shoulder.

Q. Why do penguins carry so many fish in their beaks?
A. Because they haven't got any pockets.

Q. Why did the penguin cross the ice?
A. To go with the floe!

Q. What do penguins put in salads?
A. Iceberg lettuce!

Q. What do penguins wear on their heads?
A. Ice caps!

Q. How do penguins make the perfect pancake?
A. With their flippers!

Q. What do you call fifty penguins at the North Pole?
A. Really lost, because penguins live in the Southern Hemisphere!

Q. Why are penguins good racing drivers?
A. Because they're always in pole position!

Q. How does a penguin build its house?
A. Igloos it together!

Q. Why don't you see penguins in Great Britain?
A. Because they're afraid of Wales!

Q. What do polar bears eat for lunch?
A. Iceburgers!

Q. What's white, furry and shaped like a tooth?
A. A molar bear!

Q. Why do polar bears have fur coats?
A. Because they would look silly in ski jackets!

Q. What weighs two tonnes and rolls around?
A. A walrus on a skateboard!

Ridiculous Reptiles

Q. What snake is the best at maths?
A. An adder.

Q. In which river are you sure to find snakes?
A. The Hiss-issippi river!

Q. Did you hear about the snake's love letter?
A. He sealed it with a hiss.

Q. Why did the snake laugh so hard she started to cry?
A. She thought the joke was hiss-terical.

Q. What's the wrong time to reason with a snake?
A. When it's throwing a hissy fit.

Q. Why don't snakes need to weigh themselves?
A. Because they have their own scales.

Q. What kind of snake keeps its car the cleanest?
A. A window viper!

Q. What do two snakes do after they argue?
A. Hiss and make up!

Q. What do snakes use to cut paper?
A. Scissss-ors!

Q. What do you call a snake that builds things?
A. A boa constructor!

Q. What do you call taking a selfie with a rattlesnake?
A. A missss-take.

Q. What is a snake's favourite subject?
A. Hissss-tory!

Q. **Why did the turtle cross the road?**
A. **To get to the shell station!**

Q. What kind of photos does a turtle take?
A. Shellfies.

Q. **What does a turtle do on its birthday?**
A. **It shell-ebrates!**

Q. What kind of jokes do turtles tell?
A. Absolutely shell-arious ones!

Q. What do you call a turtle that flies?
A. A shell-icopter!

Q. What do you call a truckload of
tortoises crashing into a trainload of
terrapins?
A. A turtle disaster.

Q. What do turtles use to
communicate?
A. A shell-ephone!

Q. What's the most popular name for girl turtles?
A. Shelly.

Q. What's the most popular name for boy turtles?
A. Sheldon.

Q. Why don't crocodiles like fast food?
A. Because they can't catch it!

Q. What do you call a crocodile in a vest?
A. An investigator.

Knock, knock.
Who's there?
Alligator.
Alligator who?
Alligator for her birthday was a card!

Q. What do you call a crocodile with GPS?
A. A navigator.

Q. Why are crocodiles so funny?
A. Their wit is as sharp as their teeth!

Q. What is a crocodile's favourite card game?
A. Snap.

Q. What do you call a lizard that loves hip hop?
A. A rap-tile!

Knock, knock.
Who's there?
Iguana.
Iguana who?
Iguana hold your hand!

Amusing Amphibians

Q. What do you call an amphibian in disguise?
A. Infrognito!

Q. What happens when a frog's car breaks down?
A. He gets toad away.

Q. Where do frogs like to sit?
A. On toadstools.

Q. What does a frog have for lunch?
A. French flies and a diet croak!

Q. Why are frogs so happy?
A. Because they eat everything that bugs them.

Q. What's white on the outside and green on the inside?
A. A frog sandwich!

Q. What do you say to a hitchhiking frog?
A. Hop in!

Q. **What does a frog say when he sees something great?**
A. **Toadly awesome!**

Q. Why did the frog croak?
A. Because he ate a poisonous fly!

Q. **Why did the frog go to the hospital?**
A. **He needed a hop-peration!**

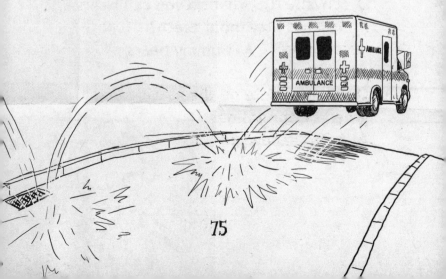

Wacky Woodland

Q. What international sporting event for wild boars is held every four years?
A. The Olym-pigs!

Q. Why didn't the teddy bear eat his lunch?
A. Because he was stuffed!

Q. What do you call bears without ears?
A. Bs

Q. What do you call bears without teeth?
A. Gummy bears

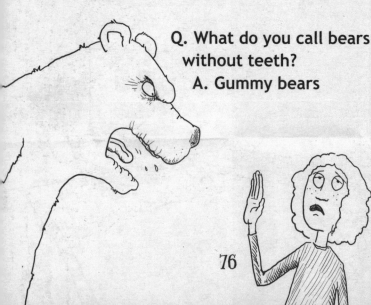

Q. Why do badgers like old movies?
A. Because they're in black and white.

Knock, knock.
Who's there?
Hoo.
Hoo who?
You sound just like an owl!

Q. What type of books do owls love?
A. Hootdunits!

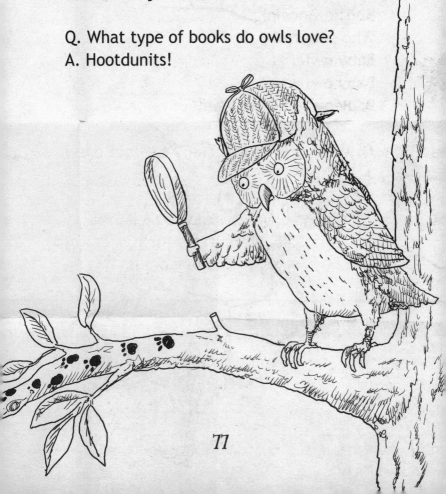

Q. Why do owls never go on dates in the rain?
A. They find it too wet to woo!

Q. Why do owls like to live in pairs?
A. They don't like to be owl by themselves.

Knock, knock.
Who's there?
Baby owl.
Baby owl who?
Baby owl see you later.

Q. What's an owl's favourite party food?
A. Mice cream

Q. What do you call an owl with a sore throat?
A. A bird that doesn't give a hoot!

Q. What do you call an owl with a low voice?
A. A growl!

Q. Why did the owl, 'owl?
A. Because the woodpecker would peck 'er!

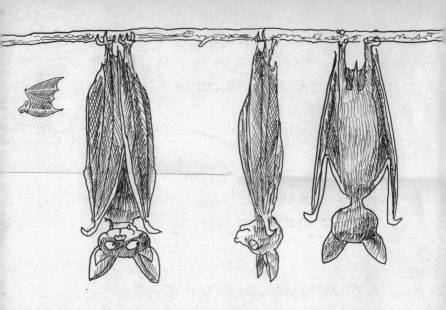

Q. What did the bat say to his friend?
A. Wanna hang out?

Q. What do bats do at night?
A. Aerobatics!

Q. What did the baby mouse say when
he saw a bat for the first time?
A. Mummy, I've just seen an angel.

Q. What is the first thing that bats learn
at school?
A. The alpha-bat.

Q. What do you call a bat inside a bell?
A. A dingbat.

Q. How do bats fly without bumping into anything?
A. They use their wing mirrors.

Q. What did the bat say to the vampire?
A. You suck!

Q. What is a bat's favourite song?
A. "Raindrops keep falling on my feet"!

Knock, knock.
Who's there?
Bat.
Bat who?
Bat you'll never guess!

Q. Who did Bambi invite to his birthday party?
A. His nearest and deer-est friends.

Q. How much is an American deer?
A. Just a buck!

Q. How do you ride a deer?
A. You hang on for deer life.

Q. What do you call a deer with no eyes?
A. I have no i-deer.

Q. Why do male deer need braces?
A. Because they have buckteeth!

Mad Mash-ups

Q. What do you get if you cross a dog with a cat?
A. An animal that chases itself!

Q. **What do you get if you cross a dog with an iguana?**
A. **A dog that can lick you from the other side of the road!**

Q. What do you get if you cross a sheepdog with a rose?
A. A collie-flower!

Q. **What do you get if you cross a cat with a lemon?**
A. **A sourpuss!**

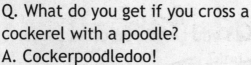

Q. What do you get if you cross a cockerel with a poodle?
A. Cockerpoodledoo!

Q. What do you get if you cross a fish with an elephant?
A. Swimming trunks!

Q. What do you get if you cross a dog with a lion?
A. A terrified postman!

Q. What do you get if you cross a bear with a skunk?
A. Winnie the PHEW!

Q. What do you get if you cross a hedgehog and a giraffe?
A. A three-metre toothbrush.

Q. What do you get if you cross a kangaroo and an elephant?
A. Giant footprints all across Australia!

Q. What do you get if you cross a spider and an elephant?
A. I'm not sure, but if you see one walking on the ceiling then run before it collapses!

Q. **What do you get if you cross a cow with a camel?**
A. **Lumpy milkshakes!**

Q. What do you get if you cross a chicken with a dog?
A. Pooched eggs!

Q. **What do you get if you cross an octopus and a cow?**
A. **An animal that can milk itself!**

Q. What do you get if you cross a snake
with a pie?
A. A pie-thon!

Q. What do you get if you cross some
ants with some ticks?
A. All sorts of antics.

Q. What do you get if you cross a rabbit
with a leaf blower?
A. A hare dryer!

Q. What do you get if you cross a tiger
with a sheep?
A. A stripy jumper!

Q. What do you get if you cross an angry sheep with a moody cow?
A. An animal that's in a baaaad mooood.

Q. What do you get if you cross a sheep with a porcupine?
A. An animal that knits its own socks.

Q. What do you get if you cross a crocodile with a flower?
A. I don't know, but I wouldn't recommend smelling it!

Q. What do you get if you cross a cat with an owl?
A. Meowls.

Q. What do you get if you cross a kangaroo with a sheep?
A. A woolly jumper.

Q. What do you get if you cross a penguin with a zebra?
A. A striped dinner jacket!

Q. What do you get if you cross a chicken with a bell?
A. An alarm cluck.

Q. What do you get if you cross a cow with a goat?
A. A coat!

Q. What do you get when you cross a rabbit with a goat?
A. A hare in your milk!

Q. What do you get when you cross a giraffe with a teacher?
A. A person that everyone looks up to.

Q. What do you get when you cross a crocodile and a rooster?
A. A crocadoodledoo.

Q. What do you get when you cross an owl and an oyster?
A. Pearls of wisdom.

Q. What do you get when you cross a turtle and a porcupine?
A. A slowpoke.

Gigglers

SCHOOL JOKES

OVER **300** JOKES

SIR, THE DOG ATE MY HOMEWORK

Gigglers

DiSGUSTiNG JOKES

OVER 300 JOKES

Gigglers

CHRISTMAS
JOKES

OVER **300** JOKES

Gigglers

SPORTY JOKES

OVER 300 JOKES